When Zeppelins Flew

Editor and Designer: Charles Mikolaycak   Assistant: Carole Kismaric   Writers: Peter Wood and Edmund White

When Zeppelins Flew

in pictures by Ken Dallison

TIME-LIFE BOOKS, New York

Previous page: Count Ferdinand von Zeppelin (1838-1917), inventor of the rigid airship

The First Flight. On July 2, 1900, spectators gathered in boats and along the shore of Lake Constance in southern Germany. As they watched, a steamboat tugged on a long line that reached inside a huge floating hangar. Slowly a silver object shaped like an enormous sausage began to emerge from the shed. Everyone gasped at its size. From tip to tail it was 419 feet long—bigger than many ocean-going ships. Yet despite its length, it was extremely light because its frame was built of the new metal called aluminum. Inside the hull, which hovered a few feet above the water, were 17 gas bags filled with hydrogen. Mounted on struts that held them clear of the craft were two propellers attached to small engines. In open-air gondolas attached to the bottom of the airship rode five men, including the inventor of the craft, Count Ferdinand von Zeppelin.

Once clear of the hangar the Zeppelin, as it was called, was maneuvered into the wind by the little tugboat. Some observers were afraid that a spark from the tug or the airship's engines themselves might ignite the highly explosive hydrogen gas and turn the whole ship into a flaming mass. But they forgot their fears the moment the tug picked up speed and began to pull its huge burden into the air like a kite. When the airship was cut loose, it rose still higher until it was nearly a quarter of a mile above the lake. Its two tiny engines sputtered and choked as they barely moved the Zeppelin against the strong winds that were blowing. But, to the astonishment of nearly everyone below, the ship stayed in the air for 17 minutes and flew more than three miles.

Next page: Sightseers come out in boats to watch an early Zeppelin emerge from its floating hangar on Lake Constance.

8 A tailless Zeppelin of 1900, the LZ-1, was the first to fly.

Count Zeppelin had first become interested in airships when, as a young German cavalry officer 35 years before, he had been sent to the United States to observe the progress of the Civil War. While in this country he rode for the first time in a gas balloon and recognized the many possibilities of lighter-than-air craft—also called airships, since they float in air rather than fly like an airplane or one of today's rockets.

It was in lighter-than-air craft that men first flew. In 1783, nearly a century before the Count made his flight, two Frenchmen rose over the city of Paris in a wickerwork basket attached to a cloth and paper balloon filled with hot air. They flew for 25 minutes before the air cooled and they settled to earth again. The balloonists who followed the Frenchmen into the sky made a few improvements. One was to replace hot air, which loses lift as it cools, with hydrogen, the lightest of all gases. Even though hydrogen can be dangerous, many early balloonists used it without accident, climbing to heights of several thousand feet and making flights that lasted many hours. But they soon saw that if any kind of aircraft was to be really useful a pilot must be able to steer it, rather than simply drift with the wind. Many men in many countries worked on the problem of the "dirigible," as a lighter-than-air craft capable of being directed is called.

It was not until he retired from the army in 1890 that the Count was able to devote

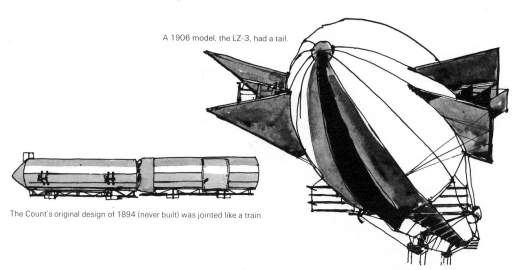

A 1906 model, the LZ-3, had a tail.

The Count's original design of 1894 (never built) was jointed like a train.

himself to the task. His idea was to build a large dirigible airship, powered by motor-driven propellers. But carrying out the idea was not so easy. To lift the weight of the motors and a crew, such a ship would have to hold far more gas than any balloon yet flown. In fact, many balloons, attached together, would be needed. To give them a shape that could fly against the wind Count Zeppelin thought they could be placed together inside some sort of a long, streamlined framework. There were two advantages to such a design. First, by having many balloons the ship could stay aloft even if one or two of them started leaking or collapsed. Second, the ship would always keep its streamlined, maneuverable shape even if it began to lose gas.

In 1894, the Count made a model of his first "air cruiser" *(far left below)*. He believed that the invention would be of great value to his country, and he asked the German government for the money to build it. Count Zeppelin was granted a patent on his design, but a panel of experts, after examining his plans, decided that the government should not invest in such a radical scheme. So the Count used his own money to assemble a group of engineers and workmen to build his first ship.

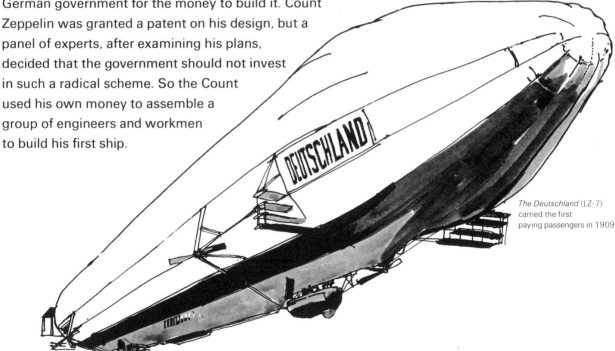

The *Deutschland* (LZ-7) carried the first paying passengers in 1909.

10   Although Count Zeppelin's first dirigible flight, on that summer day in 1900, had lasted for more than a quarter of an hour, it had not been a complete success. The experiment had ended abruptly when the frail skeleton of the ship buckled, the rudder ropes fouled and there was a breakdown in the mechanism of shifting weights with which the Zeppelin was steered up and down. The ship was totally out of control, the men on board helpless. But instead of crashing into the lake, as an airplane would have, it slowly floated down to the surface of the water, landing on top of a buoy. One of the gas cells was punctured, but the crew suffered not the slightest scratch. The Count had his ship repaired and a few months later flew it twice more without mishap, but, as on the first flight, the dirigible made too little headway against the wind. Its two motors —each of which had roughly the power of one of today's medium-sized marine outboard motors—were simply not strong enough. But by the time the Count made this discovery he had run out of money. Still unable to get the government to help him, he was forced to let his entire staff go and to sell the Zeppelin's engines and its aluminum framework for scrap. People were sure that his experiment had failed.

Ludwig Dürr, who became Zeppelin's chief construction engineer, started working with the Count in 1899.

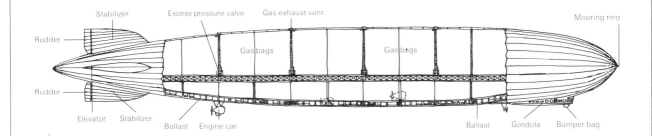

All Zeppelins, from the first experimental models to later airliners like the *Graf Zeppelin (above),* used the same basic principles to fly. A Zeppelin moved through the air much as a fish moves through water. Like water, air resists movement through it. So the first Zeppelins were built with pointed bows, like the head of a fish, to cut easily through the air, and their sterns were streamlined so that the air would flow smoothly past the hull *(top diagram below)* instead of curling back to create turbulence or "drag" that would slow the ship *(bottom diagram).*

The Count's first airship used a weight hung from a track beneath the hull to direct it up or down. Pulled forward, the weight caused the bow to

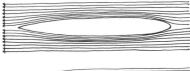

dip; pulled back, it caused the bow to rise. But in operation this device proved clumsy. Later Zeppelins, like airplanes, made use instead of movable flaps,

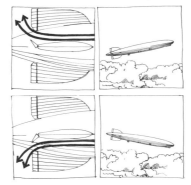

called elevators, attached to horizontal tail fins. With engines driving the airship ahead and the elevators turned up, air pushing against the elevators caused the tail of the dirigible to dip and the bow to lift *(top diagram above).* When the elevators were turned down, the tail lifted and the bow dropped *(bottom diagram).* Other flaps, called rudders, attached to the vertical tail fins, were used to steer the Zeppelin to the left and right, just like the rudder on a boat.

Another way to make a Zeppelin rise or sink was to change its weight. On take-off, Zeppelins carried large amounts of water in ballast tanks fore and aft. If a commander wanted to climb rapidly he would drop ballast from both tanks. Or he might drop ballast from one tank only in order to level his ship *(diagram below).* To descend, he would release gas from the cells, a process called "valving off." As the ship went higher, the air became thinner, exerting less pressure on the gas bags so that the gas inside expanded. At very high altitudes the gas in a Zeppelin expanded beyond the capacity of the bags to hold it, causing the ship to "valve off" automatically

through safety valves. If the commander did not then drop ballast the ship would sink. Whenever possible, however, a Zeppelin commander relied on elevators and rudder alone to maneuver so as not to waste precious lifting gas.

12   Despite his first setback, Count Zeppelin was determined to continue building airships. He believed that Germany could use a whole fleet of them to carry passengers and mail around Europe. Others felt that, in case of war, his dirigibles could be valuable weapons against an enemy. To finance another ship, a special lottery was arranged with the help of the King of the local State of Württemberg, who was sympathetic to the Count's cause. After the prize money was paid to the lottery winners, 124,000 marks (about $30,000) were left for the Count to build a second airship.

The new Zeppelin contained many improvements. It had a stronger body, and in place of the weight-shifting device it had tail fins that could be tilted up or down to make the ship descend or rise. Most important, it had much more powerful engines. This second

A lottery ticket used to raise money for the Count's work

ship flew successfully, but afterward it was destroyed in a violent storm. Refusing to give up, the Count scraped together the very last of his personal fortune and built a third dirigible, the LZ-3. (This stood for *Luftschiff,* meaning "airship"; *Zeppelin,* designating the builder; *Number 3,* the third one to be built. All later Zeppelins used this code, up to the last one, the LZ-130.) The LZ-3 flew so well that everyone in Germany, including the nation's ruler, Kaiser Wilhelm II, became fascinated with the big silver ships. Germans started smoking "Zeppelin" cigarettes, wearing "Zeppelin" coats and even

After a triumphant flight to Berlin in 1909, the elderly Count Zeppelin is met by the German Kaiser himself *(center).*

14 eating pastries shaped like Zeppelins. The government decided that if the Count could build a fourth ship and fly it without landing for 24 hours, they would finance his work.

On August 4, 1908, the Count climbed aboard his fourth airship, the LZ-4, to make the test. Newspapermen from many countries had come to report the flight. Members of the Kaiser's government flew as observers. Although the ship was forced to make a brief landing to repair an engine, it did stay in the air a total of more than 24 hours, and the officials aboard were highly impressed. It seemed certain that the government would buy the Zeppelin. But during a thunderstorm the very next afternoon, the airship was blown from its mooring, burst into flame and was completely destroyed.

The disaster, however, proved to be a blessing in disguise. The course of the LZ-4 had been as carefully followed by the German people as any present-day flight into space. The Count became a national hero, and all Germans took pride in his achievements. They swamped him with mail containing thousands of small contributions for him to continue his work. The Kaiser was so enthusiastic that he proclaimed the Count the "greatest German of the Twentieth Century." Honored and well-financed at last, Count Zeppelin, in 1909, set up a dirigible passenger service between several major German cities. The first ship, the *Deutschland* (LZ-7) crashed in the Teutoburg Forest after seven flights. But later Zeppelins proved so safe and efficient that when World War I broke out in 1914, the German government had already decided to use them as major weapons.

Spectators stare at the wreckage of an early Zeppelin, which lies crumpled like a huge paper bag on a German hillside.

16 The Zeppelin at War. In 1914, Germany faced three powerful enemies: France, Russia and Great Britain. The British had the most powerful navy in the world and were able to blockade German ports and hold off German attacks on England. The German High Command realized, however, that the British had no effective defense against a Zeppelin, which could be armed with bombs and attack under the cover of darkness. In 1914 most British airplanes had tiny engines and required almost an hour to climb to 10,000 feet, the cruising height of a Zeppelin.

At first, the German Kaiser hesitated to order the raids. He knew that despite every precaution taken to bomb only military targets civilians would certainly be killed and the world would label the Germans as barbarians. But there was no other way to strike at the island fortress, and he finally gave in to the pleas of his High Command. Early in 1915 the first air raids in history began. The raids were usually carried out on nights when the moon was new or covered by clouds. For more than two centuries Britain had not been invaded, but suddenly citizens of London and coastal cities were terrorized by the sound of sirens shrieking at night and bombs bursting all around them.

The most destructive raid of the war took place on the night of September 8, 1915, when Heinrich Mathy, commanding the L-13, set fires in the heart of London. (The German Navy numbered its airships in the order in which they were commissioned. Mathy's ship, the Navy's 13th Zeppelin, was actually the LZ-45.) All of London's 26 antiaircraft guns and

20 searchlights were aimed at Mathy, but the L-13, flying two miles above the city, was well out of their range. One British witness angrily reported: "As seen from below, the airship gave an impression of absolute calm and absence of hurry." This single Zeppelin bombed warehouses, a train station, a bank, an apartment building and a public square, killing 22 people and causing millions of dollars worth of damage.

A less spectacular but far more practical use for the Zeppelins was as scouts at sea. Germany's navy was much smaller and weaker than Britain's and to protect their fleet the Germans sent airships out ahead to look for enemy ships and to radio back warnings. Other Zeppelins were used as spotters to help keep German submarine lanes cleared of mines, the explosive devices which the British planted underwater to try to prevent the U-boats from reaching the open seas. The black lines in the upper right corner of the German map below trace the routes patrolled by the Zeppelins. When they spotted a mine they would radio to a German mine sweeper to come and destroy it, while watching to see that a British warship was not lurking over the horizon to pounce on the small craft.

When Zeppelins were not raiding Britain or protecting the German fleet, they staged attacks on Germany's other enemies. In fact, the first Zeppelin action of the war was the bombardment of several French cities; Paris itself was attacked several times, as were cities in countries as far away as Romania and Greece.

A German map, entitled "Zeppelin Raids Against England," sums up the early wartime activities of the Zeppelins. Dotted lines trace bombing raids over England; heavy black lines show patrol routes at sea. Zeppelin bases in Germany (upper right) are marked by circled dots.

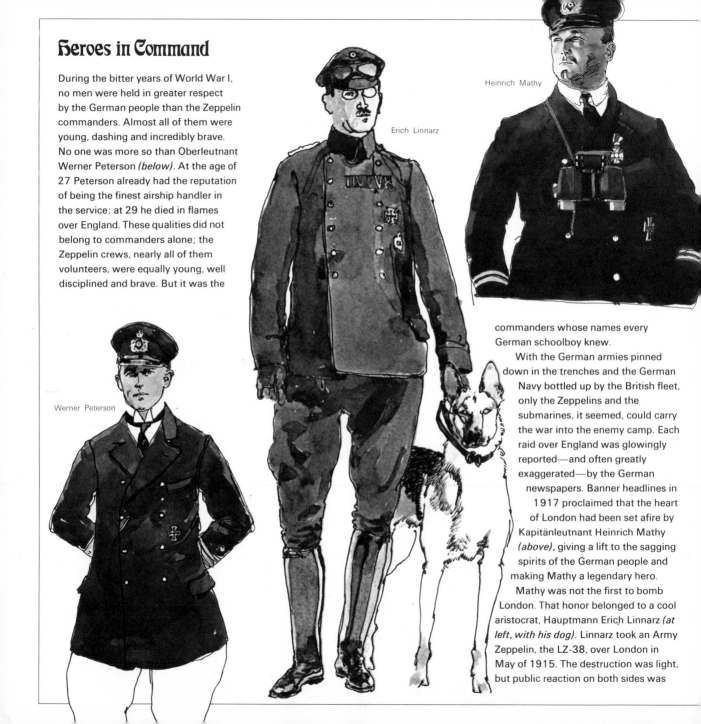

Heroes in Command

During the bitter years of World War I, no men were held in greater respect by the German people than the Zeppelin commanders. Almost all of them were young, dashing and incredibly brave. No one was more so than Oberleutnant Werner Peterson *(below)*. At the age of 27 Peterson already had the reputation of being the finest airship handler in the service; at 29 he died in flames over England. These qualities did not belong to commanders alone; the Zeppelin crews, nearly all of them volunteers, were equally young, well disciplined and brave. But it was the

Heinrich Mathy

Erich Linnarz

Werner Peterson

commanders whose names every German schoolboy knew.

With the German armies pinned down in the trenches and the German Navy bottled up by the British fleet, only the Zeppelins and the submarines, it seemed, could carry the war into the enemy camp. Each raid over England was glowingly reported—and often greatly exaggerated—by the German newspapers. Banner headlines in 1917 proclaimed that the heart of London had been set afire by Kapitänleutnant Heinrich Mathy *(above)*, giving a lift to the sagging spirits of the German people and making Mathy a legendary hero.

Mathy was not the first to bomb London. That honor belonged to a cool aristocrat, Hauptmann Erich Linnarz *(at left, with his dog)*. Linnarz took an Army Zeppelin, the LZ-38, over London in May of 1915. The destruction was light, but public reaction on both sides was profound: England, he had proved, could be attacked! On a later raid, the proud Linnarz was driven off his target by antiaircraft fire. He was so enraged that he scribbled a note on his calling card, attached it to a weighted streamer and hurled it out of the open gondola. "You English," the note read, "we have come, and we will come again soon, to kill or cure! [signed] Linnarz."

The Army had the distinction of bombing London first, but it was the Navy that carried out most of the raids across the North Sea. The man commanding the Navy's Zeppelin force was Fregattenkapitän Peter Strasser, shown standing at the far right. He was, by all accounts, a brilliant, inspiring —and decidedly stubborn—Leader of Airships. No one under his command had anything but praise for Strasser, even after the terrible losses that the Naval airships suffered late in the war. Strasser was sure that Zeppelins offered "a certain means of victoriously ending the war." But British planes and antiaircraft guns had been so much improved by 1917 that raids over England had become almost suicide missions. Nevertheless, Strasser continued to order his ships out—and continued to fly with them himself on at least one raid a month. On one such flight, near the end of the war, Strasser paid for his stubborn faith in airships with his life *(see page 28)*. Many brave commanders and crews had died before him, the famous Heinrich Mathy among them. Mathy was shot down over England

only seven days after Peterson; an officer who had flown with him wrote, "It was the aeroplane firing the incendiary bullet that brought about his downfall, and with him the life and soul of our airship service went out too."

Of the commanders shown here, only two survived the war: Linnarz and Kapitänleutnant Horst von Buttlar-Brandenfels, seated below with his executive officer Oberleutnant Hans von Schiller standing behind him. Like many other Navy men who had flown airships during the war, Von Schiller continued in the Zeppelin service afterward. Eventually he became the commanding officer of one of the last great peacetime airships, the *Graf Zeppelin*.

Peter Strasser

Hans von Schiller

Horst von Buttlar-Brandenfels

A Fighting Zeppelin

The Zeppelin shown below is of the type used by the Germans to bomb England during the latter part of the war. Called a "height climber," it was designed to operate at altitudes of more than 20,000 feet or nearly four miles, higher than existing airplanes were able to go. The height climbers were painted black underneath to make them harder to see at night from the ground. They held nearly two million cubic feet of hydrogen and could carry about 7,000 pounds of bombs. This ship was 644 feet long and was manned by a crew of 20. Its five engines drove it at a top speed of close to 70 miles per hour.

The Germans were so sure that the British planes could not reach them that they built the first Zeppelins of this type without machine-gun stations. However, guns were added later when British planes were improved. The men

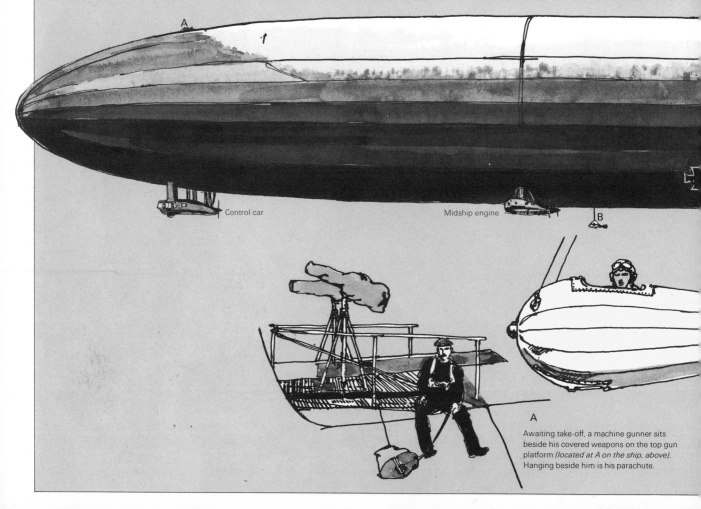

Control car

Midship engine

A

Awaiting take-off, a machine gunner sits beside his covered weapons on the top gun platform *(located at A on the ship, above).* Hanging beside him is his parachute.

who manned the gun stations faced terrible wind and cold, crouched all alone on their tiny open platforms in the thin upper atmosphere. The height climbers occasionally carried "spy cars" in which an observer connected to the ship by telephone was lowered to direct the dropping of bombs. However, the added weight of the car and its cable so limited the bomb load a Zeppelin could carry that it was not often used.

All German Navy Zeppelins flew this flag at the tips of their tails. It bears the German eagle and Iron Cross on a field of black, red and white.

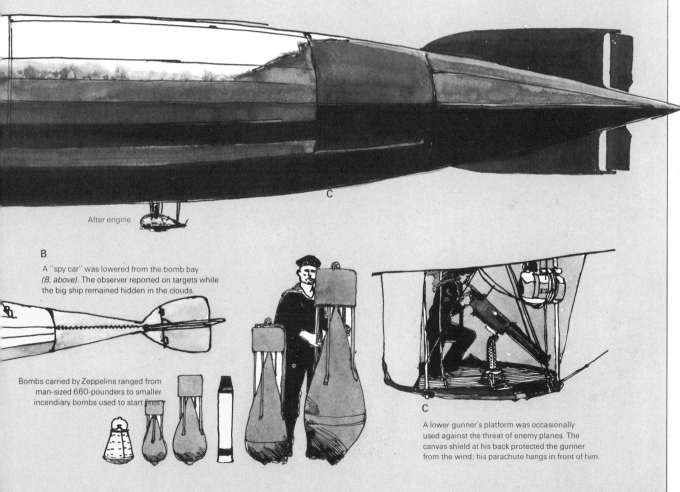

After engine

B

A "spy car" was lowered from the bomb bay *(B, above)*. The observer reported on targets while the big ship remained hidden in the clouds.

Bombs carried by Zeppelins ranged from man-sized 660-pounders to smaller incendiary bombs used to start fires.

C

A lower gunner's platform was occasionally used against the threat of enemy planes. The canvas shield at his back protected the gunner from the wind; his parachute hangs in front of him.

At the beginning of World War I the airplane was a frail toy and the Zeppelin was the undisputed master of the skies. As the war progressed, however, both the airplane and its weapons were improved, and those improvements spelled an end to the Zeppelin as an effective instrument of war. In 1915, when the Zeppelins made their first raids on England, British defenses were disorganized and inadequate; 20 Zeppelins flew over the British coast and killed 208 people, and only one Zeppelin was downed. Frightened by these losses, the English soon began to improve their defenses. They replaced their old antiaircraft guns with more accurate French weapons. They reorganized their airplane squadrons, equipping them with faster, higher-flying planes that could fire incendiary bullets. Just one incendiary bullet, properly aimed, was usually all it took to turn a hydrogen-filled Zeppelin into a flaming coffin.

Airship crews did their best not to think too much about these new dangers. One commander, Joachim Breithaupt, told what it was like to be in a Zeppelin over London in 1916: "The picture we saw was indescribably beautiful—shrapnel bursting all around (though rather uncomfortably near us), our own bombs bursting, and the flashes from the antiaircraft batteries below. On either hand the other airships, which, like us, were caught in the rays of the searchlights, were clearly recognizable. And over us the starlit sky." A few weeks later Breithaupt's airship was riddled by some of that shrapnel and he and his crew taken prisoner, the first victims of the stiffening English defenses.

The "Count of Hartlepool"

To succeed in their wartime missions, Zeppelin commanders needed quick wits and steel nerves. To survive, they needed luck. No one knew this better than Kapitänleutnant Martin Dietrich, a career naval officer who had volunteered for airship service at the beginning of the war. Between 1915 and 1918, Dietrich commanded five Zeppelins; he lost only one—and that without the loss of a single life. He knew he was lucky, and he was not ashamed of being superstitious about it. Dietrich always flew the same flag from each ship he commanded. By the end of the war nothing was left of it but a tattered stub *(right)*. Nor would he change his hat; he wore the same one on every mission despite the fact that part way through the war the airship uniform was changed. And he never looked at any of the good luck pieces, like the oak leaves at the right, that were sent to him by the hundreds.

Dietrich's finest moment came on the terrible night just after Christmas in 1916 when he lost the L-38. Sent on a risky mission to raid Russia, he was caught in a fierce snowstorm over the eastern Baltic Sea. The temperature at his altitude of 10,000 feet was 8 degrees below zero. Snow weighed down the ship: ice, striking the spinning propellers, was flung through the hull, puncturing the gas cells. Dietrich turned back. And then began a battle with the elements that no man aboard the L-38 will ever forget.

The flag Dietrich flew from five ships

An oak-leaf cluster, one of many tokens sent to Dietrich by the German people

All ballast and most bombs had already been dropped. The ship, still hundreds of pounds heavy, flew with its nose tilted 15 degrees up in the air, its tail dipping into the freezing sea, its engines faltering. To help level the ship, crewmen carried the remaining bombs forward. Finally, after four hours, the L-38 managed to reach the German-held coast. Dietrich chose to land in a forest, where the trees cradled the weight of the stricken ship. Had he landed in an open field instead, the heavy ship would have crushed its own gondolas, possibly killing many of the crew.

Dietrich showed the same cool judgment two years later in a raid over the British city of Hartlepool. This time he was commanding the L-42, —pictured at the right fighting off an attack from two enemy planes. In the gondola with Dietrich *(pointing)* are his executive officer, the elevator and rudder operators and two machine gunners. The L-42 had set out with two other ships to bomb factories in England. When the wind suddenly changed, Leader of Airships Peter Strasser recalled the raid. Dietrich, however, was already in sight of the coast of England when he received the signal, and he chose to ignore it, risking a court-martial. Later he said, "I knew the raid had to be a success. If I had failed, I would have had to quit the service." Dietrich flew on alone and dropped 21 bombs on Hartlepool, destroying many buildings. When he got home, instead of reprimanding him, Strasser jokingly named Dietrich the "Count of Hartlepool."

26 By 1916 British airplanes had become more than a match for the raiding Zeppelins. Refusing to accept this fact, the Germans increased the number of airship raids, but they caused much less damage than they had in 1915. More seriously for the Germans, six Zeppelins were destroyed and 95 crew members were killed. Machine guns, firing from English airplanes, were causing most of the losses.

The airplanes, however, were able to reach a height of only about 13,000 feet. In order to escape the planes, the Germans relied on their "height climbers," the huge Zeppelins that could reach ceilings of more than 20,000 feet. But at such great heights the crews faced new problems. The air was so thin that men were forced to sniff oxygen to keep from passing out. Terrible cold numbed their bodies and created all sorts of mechanical difficulties that sometimes knocked out the engines. Worst of all, violent storms and unpredictable winds often raged at these high altitudes, quite independently of the weather on the ground.

Because the height climbers often flew above the clouds, where landmarks could not be seen, navigation became a matter of guesswork and sighting targets was often impossible. Time and again Strasser's Zeppelins became hopelessly lost, and more than one disappeared at sea without a trace. As a result of these difficulties, the Germans were able to stage only 39 raids against England after 1916; little of value was destroyed, and London was bombed by a Zeppelin only once.

London is set ablaze by Heinrich Mathy in 1916. Searchlights pinpoint the raider, but the city's guns cannot reach him.

The Last Raid

One evening towards the end of the war, three Zeppelins heading for London were met by a new, high-flying British biplane. The pilot, Major Egbert Cadbury, described the fateful moment: "We climbed to 16,400 feet and I attacked. My observer [Captain Robert Leckie] trained his gun on the bow of the airship. . . . The ZPT [an explosive bullet] was seen to blow a great hole in the fabric and a fire started. . . . The Zeppelin raised her bows as if in an effort to escape, then plunged seaward, a blazing mass." Down with the airship and its entire crew went Peter Strasser, the German Navy's Leader of Airships. Until that moment, Strasser had stubbornly believed that British planes and guns could not reach his highflying craft. The other two ships escaped, but this defeat marked the last Zeppelin raid of the war.

Major Cadbury

Captain Leckie

30 **Building a Luxury Airship.** After Germany was defeated in the war, the victorious Allies prohibited the building of any more Zeppelins. Moreover, they seized for themselves those the Germans had on hand. In this division of spoils, however, the United States was left out. So it was decided that the Zeppelin Company should build one last Zeppelin. That ship, the LZ-126, was delivered to the Naval Air Station at Lakehurst, New Jersey, in 1924. It was christened the *Los Angeles* and flown by the U.S. Navy for years. But after building the *Los Angeles,* the Zeppelin Company was reduced to manufacturing aluminum pots and pans. All of the valuable knowledge the Germans had accumulated about airships seemed useless. Count Zeppelin himself had died in 1917 and some people claimed that his invention had died with him. They were wrong.

The man responsible for reviving Germany's airship industry was Hugo Eckener. He had been associated with the Count since the early days, and during the war he had

trained crews to man Navy dirigibles. Seven years after the end of the war, the ban against building Zeppelins was finally lifted. But the bankrupt German government could not supply the money to build the ship Eckener wanted—one large and powerful enough to carry passengers across the Atlantic. So, remembering how the German people had aided Count Zeppelin in

The control car of LZ-127 takes shape.

Right: Workmen on scaffolds crisscross the ship's giant aluminum nose cone with wire webbing.

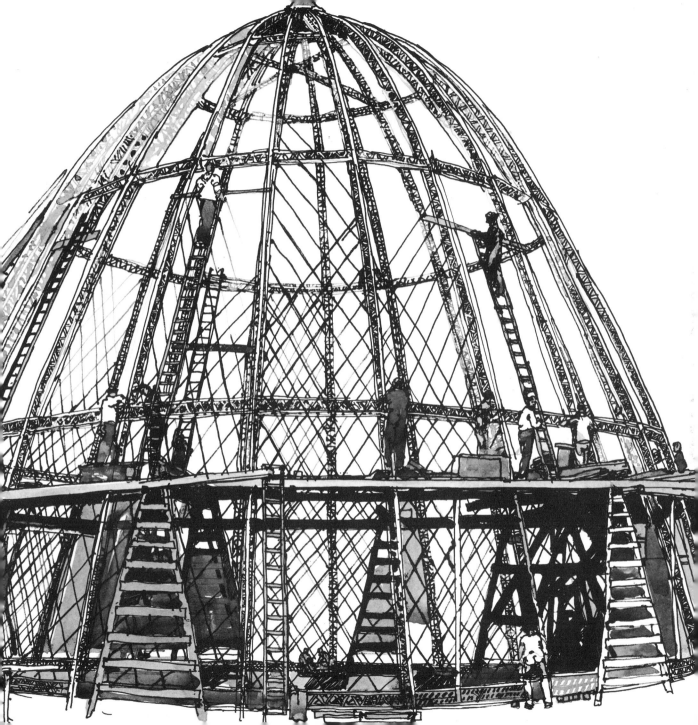

Aluminum struts
are carefully
weighed.

1909, Eckener appealed to them once more. His campaign
succeeded, and by 1927 he had received enough
contributions to begin work on the mighty LZ-127, christened
the *Graf (Count) Zeppelin* after the old man himself.

The construction of the *Graf Zeppelin* was a mammoth
project. First, more than 10 miles of girders made
of Duraluminum, a strong, light alloy of aluminum
and copper, had to be shaped for the framework. Then
workmen riveted the girders into giant rings, which they laid out
flat on the floor of a huge hangar in Friedrichshafen, beside
Lake Constance. After each of the rings was completed, it was
suspended from the hangar ceiling.

When all the rings were hanging in a row, they were joined together by girders
that ran lengthwise, from the nose of the ship to the tail. A web of wires was
added to give the hull more strength. Then a strong cotton fabric was stretched over the
metal framework, laced into place and painted a shiny, silvery color. The silver paint helped
reflect the sun's rays so that the gas inside the Zeppelin would not become hot and expand
to overflow the cells; if the Zeppelin lost too much hydrogen it would sink. The last major
task was to install the gas cells. Workmen stitched these big bags together from cotton

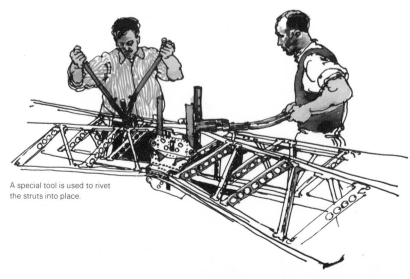

A special tool is used to rivet
the struts into place.

fabric that had been lined with airtight membranes from the intestines of oxen. About 50,000 membranes were needed to line just one gas cell, and the cost was high.

On July 8, 1928, the *Graf Zeppelin* was christened by the old Count's daughter. Ten days later the new airship made its maiden voyage over Lake Constance, the site of the Count's first flight 28 years before. The ship was powered by five engines, each mounted in a separate gondola held clear of the outside of the hull by struts—two engines on each side and one underneath near the tail. Together they provided the power to drive the 776-foot-long dirigible at a top speed of 80 miles an hour. Under the nose of the ship protruded the main gondola, the front of which contained the control room. From this large-windowed "bridge" the ship's captain, Hugo Eckener, surrounded by instruments, piloted the ship. Here, too, stood the helmsmen ready to obey his commands, one manning the rudder and the other the elevator wheels. Aft of the control room were spaces for the navigator and the radio operator. Behind the control section were a lounge and 10 double cabins for the 20 passengers that the ship could carry.

The outer skin is sewn together from lengths of cotton fabric.

Next page: Inside a Zeppelin's cavernous hull, huge gasbags are suspended from cords and gradually inflated.

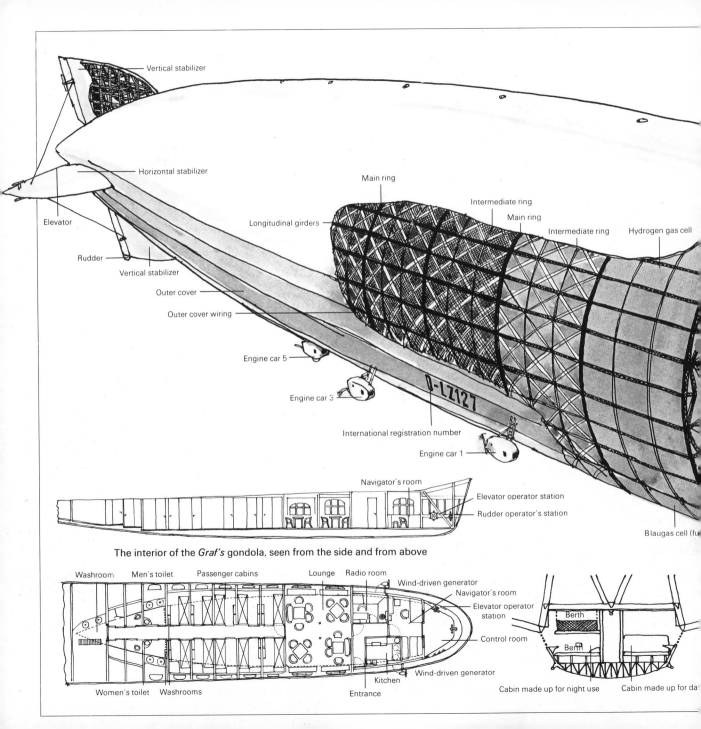

Vertical stabilizer

Horizontal stabilizer

Elevator

Rudder

Vertical stabilizer

Outer cover

Outer cover wiring

Engine car 5

Engine car 3

International registration number

Engine car 1

Main ring

Intermediate ring

Main ring

Intermediate ring

Hydrogen gas cell

Longitudinal girders

D-LZ127

Navigator's room

Elevator operator station

Rudder operator's station

Blaugas cell (fu

The interior of the *Graf's* gondola, seen from the side and from above

Washroom

Men's toilet

Passenger cabins

Lounge

Radio room

Wind-driven generator

Navigator's room

Elevator operator station

Control room

Berth

Berth

Wind-driven generator

Kitchen

Entrance

Women's toilet

Washrooms

Cabin made up for night use

Cabin made up for da

Anatomy of an Airship

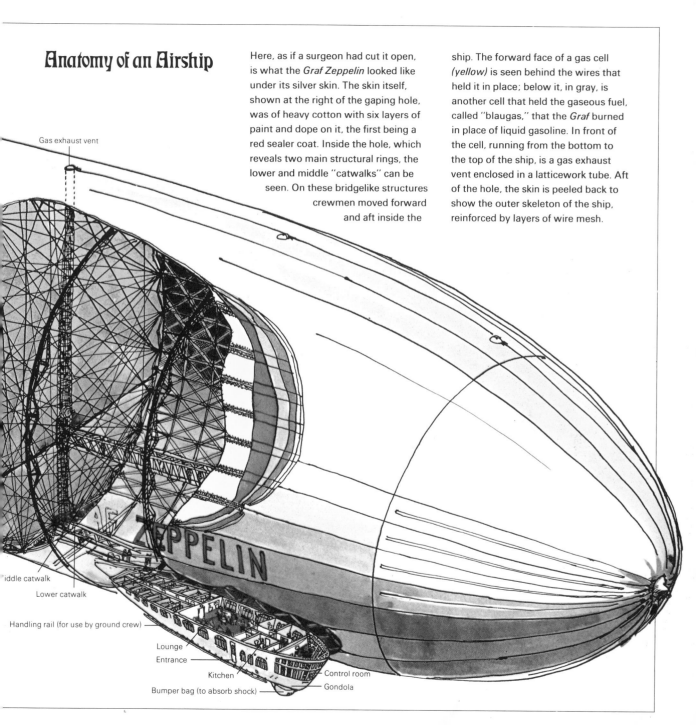

Here, as if a surgeon had cut it open, is what the *Graf Zeppelin* looked like under its silver skin. The skin itself, shown at the right of the gaping hole, was of heavy cotton with six layers of paint and dope on it, the first being a red sealer coat. Inside the hole, which reveals two main structural rings, the lower and middle "catwalks" can be seen. On these bridgelike structures crewmen moved forward and aft inside the ship. The forward face of a gas cell *(yellow)* is seen behind the wires that held it in place; below it, in gray, is another cell that held the gaseous fuel, called "blaugas," that the *Graf* burned in place of liquid gasoline. In front of the cell, running from the bottom to the top of the ship, is a gas exhaust vent enclosed in a latticework tube. Aft of the hole, the skin is peeled back to show the outer skeleton of the ship, reinforced by layers of wire mesh.

Gas exhaust vent

Middle catwalk

Lower catwalk

Handling rail (for use by ground crew)

Lounge

Entrance

Kitchen

Control room

Bumper bag (to absorb shock)

Gondola

38 **Sailing Above the Oceans, Around the World.** The *Graf Zeppelin* made its first flight across the Atlantic, from Friedrichshafen to the U.S. Naval Air Station at Lakehurst, New Jersey, in October, 1928. Aboard were 40 crewmen and 20 passengers. It was not the first time that men had flown the Atlantic; quite a few airplanes and dirigibles had gone before the *Graf*. But this particular flight captured the imagination of people everywhere; it marked the true beginning of air passenger service between Europe and America, a milestone in the air age. Soon, it seemed, for the price of a ticket anybody would be able to fly the oceans.

Before the *Graf Zeppelin* would settle into the routine of shuttling passengers back and forth across the Atlantic, making the round trip in 10 days, several adventures lay ahead. In 1929 the ship set a record by flying around the world, carrying representatives from eight countries. From an altitude of 1,000 feet over Siberia, the passengers looked down on vast, barren wastes never before seen by men. The trip, which began at Lakehurst, was interrupted by stops at Friedrichshafen, Tokyo and Los Angeles and took 21 days. The next year the *Graf* carried an international expedition of scientists to the Arctic to gather data on the weather and geography of that remote region.

With these epic flights behind it, the *Graf* began making scheduled runs between Germany and Brazil. Brazil was chosen as a destination because of the long time—two weeks—it took to reach South America by sea, and also because of the large German colony that had settled in the beautiful Brazilian city of Rio de Janeiro.

Imagine that it is the autumn of 1932, and you are about to take the *Graf Zeppelin* from its base at Friedrichshafen to Rio de Janeiro. You have been in the city since mid-afternoon and the *Graf* is scheduled to leave at 10:30 that night. The passengers are having goodbye parties and suppers with friends and relatives at the Kurgarten Hotel in town. Then, in the midst of all the festivity word comes from the airfield that an unusually strong cross wind will make it impossible to "undock" the ship from the hangar. Well, a few more hours will hurt no one. Most of the passengers have already been looking forward to making this trip for many months, some of them for years. Despite the high price of a ticket ($2,250 round trip) there is always a long waiting list for the *Graf,* which can take only 20 passengers at a time.

After a comfortable night at the Kurgarten, you are awakened early. You are served a quick breakfast, then all the passengers are driven out to the airship hangar. Provisions for the trip have been stowed on board. Your baggage—strictly limited to 65 pounds per passenger—is tucked under your berth in one of the 10 double cabins. A few more last-minute pieces of mail are added to the thousands of airmail letters and cards already aboard. The delay of the night before is forgotten in the excitement around you. The call goes out to board the ship, which is still inside the hangar, and saying their last goodbyes, passengers begin climbing the steps into the gondola.

Travel folder and baggage sticker
used for the Rio flight

The sandbags that have held the giant ship down are removed and the *Graf* rises a foot or two, putting a slight strain on the ropes held by the ground crew of 300 men. High above, it seems that the top of the Zeppelin will surely scrape the beams that support the hangar's huge roof. But all has been calculated perfectly. The *Graf*, in fact, was built to fit this hangar exactly, a fact that limited its size and is the reason why it can carry so few passengers.

Using a whistle, an officer directs the men to "walk" the ship out of the hangar. It takes nearly 15 minutes for the ground crew to ease the huge craft into the open. This is one of the most critical moments of the whole trip. A sudden, unexpected gust of wind could well smash the frail hull against the hangar door. Captain Ernst Lehmann, a veteran Zeppelin commander who flew many raids with the Navy during the war, walks along beside his ship, intently watching every detail of the maneuver.

Out on the field, all is ready. The treacherous wind of the night before has died down and the morning sky is bright and clear. (The favorite time for Zeppelin take-offs and landings is during the calm periods of the day around sunrise and sunset.) At last the captain climbs aboard and gives the command: "Up ship!" The lines are released and the ground handlers heave on the hand-rails attached to the control car. Like a giant bubble the ship begins to rise; the next moment the engines come to life with a roar, and the *Graf* begins to climb to cruising altitude. Next stop: Brazil.

In its hangar at Friedrichshafen, the *Graf Zeppelin* loads passengers bound for Rio, while friends gather to wave goodbye.

Like an army of ants, a ground crew of 300 men eases the huge ship out of its hangar and onto the field for take-off.

A Flight to Rio de Janeiro

For the select group of passengers aboard the *Graf*, life is luxurious and exciting. The freezing, wind-swept gondolas of the wartime Zeppelins have been replaced by a comfortable lounge and cozy private cabins. True, the passengers do not enjoy the spacious decks or grand salons found on an ocean liner. But then they are less likely to get seasick from the motion of the waves, or suffer the boredom that comes even on the best of ships after a week or so at sea.

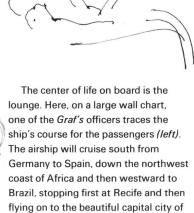

The center of life on board is the lounge. Here, on a large wall chart, one of the *Graf's* officers traces the ship's course for the passengers *(left)*. The airship will cruise south from Germany to Spain, down the northwest coast of Africa and then westward to Brazil, stopping first at Recife and then flying on to the beautiful capital city of Rio—6,250 miles in all.

At mealtime the lounge is turned into a small, elegant restaurant high in the sky *(above)*. From four tables diners look out over the panorama of southern Europe as it speeds by beneath them. Wearing his traditional white hat, the *Graf's* chef, Herr Kubis, serves the first midday meal: beef broth with marrow, dumplings, fresh Rhine salmon, roast gosling, mixed salad, pears with chocolate sauce and coffee. Kubis cooks for both crew and passengers in a small but ultra-modern kitchen off

the lounge. The stove and other appliances are electric, powered by a wind-driven generator mounted outside the galley window. (The Zeppelin service is known for its outstanding

Luftschiff Kapitän
Ernst Lehman

crews. One of the passengers' favorites on this flight is Ernst Fischbach, the young steward standing in front of the pillar in the picture. One day he will rise in the service to become a qualified pilot of airships.) After a sumptuous dinner the *Graf's* jovial captain, Ernst Lehmann, enters the lounge and entertains the passengers by playing German folk tunes on his accordion *(opposite page below).*

Later in the evening passengers retire to their cabins *(right)* where the day couches have been made up into beds by the ship's two stewards; a second bed in each cabin can be folded down from the wall above. The *Graf's* cabins boast every luxury found aboard an ocean-going ship—except running water. Water, because of its weight, is

movies instead of the view. In 1933, the idea of flying is still so new that every moment aboard the *Graf* is an adventure. And yet at the same time the trip is marvelously peaceful. The only

noise comes from the soft drone of the *Graf's* engines as they drive the ship along at a steady 70 miles per hour. From a cruising altitude of only 1,000 feet, just slightly more than the *Graf's* own length, every detail below is clearly seen—and from a viewpoint that most of the passengers have never enjoyed before *(below).* On this flight the Captain has spotted a Hanseatic Line steamer, also bound for Rio, that left Germany two weeks before the *Graf.* Circling once and then dipping low over the steamer, the Zeppelin drops a packet of the latest German newspapers, while the airborne passengers wave to the ocean travelers on deck. Then the airship rises and points its bow west again. Over the horizon, an hour away, lies the coast of Brazil and a landing in the New World.

Rio de Janeiro - America do Sul

strictly rationed on board, and the *Graf's* two bathrooms have no tub or shower.

In addition to its passengers, the *Graf* carries an important cargo of mail. Transatlantic airmail is still such a novelty that stamp collectors all over the world have sent letters and postcards, like the one above, to be postmarked aboard the famous ship.

The flight is not at all like a trip on a modern jet airplane, in which a hundred or more travelers, seated in rows, fly so high and so fast that they often watch

The Last Days of the Zeppelins. The *Graf Zeppelin* was a great success, but it could
not possibly meet the demand for air-passenger service. So in the early 1930's the
Zeppelin Company decided to build a much larger airship, the *Hindenburg* (LZ-129).
Launched on March 6, 1936, it was the most spectacular Zeppelin of all, and it seemed
about to start a new era in airship travel. Nearly the same length as the *Graf,* it was
much larger around and held twice the volume of gas. It could carry 72 passengers in
spacious quarters located inside the hull.

On the evening of May 6, 1937, the *Hindenburg* was hanging 200 feet above the
ground at Lakehurst, ready to land after its 21st routine North Atlantic crossing. The
engines were idling and mooring lines had been dropped from the airship to the ground
crew. Passengers were finishing their last-minute packing. On the horizon, lightning
flickered, marking the position of a passing thunderstorm that had delayed the landing.

The captain, Max Pruss, was worried about only one thing: the tail of the ship
seemed unusually heavy. He had ordered water ballast to be dropped from the rear, but
the dirigible still did not appear to be completely balanced. A radio announcer on the
field below was reporting to his listeners: "The motors are just holding it, just enough to
keep it from—It's broken into flames! It's flashing—flashing! It's flashing terrible! Now
it's bursting into flames and falling on the mooring mast! This is terrible! This is one of
the worst catastrophes in the world. . . . Oh, the humanity and all the passengers!"

Near the Lakehurst mooring mast, friends of passengers and sailors with long fender poles await the *Hindenburg's* arrival.

Horrified spectators run for their lives as the *Hindenburg*'s seven million cubic feet of hydrogen make the sky a burning hell.

50   At exactly 7:25 p.m. the stern of the *Hindenburg* had exploded; a minute later the entire ship was a charred wreck. No one knew exactly what had caused the explosion, and probably no one will ever know.

On the fateful day the *Hindenburg* blew up, the age of the Zeppelin came to an end. Ninety-seven people had been on board the ship; by some miracle, 62 survived. Nonetheless, death came to 13 passengers, 22 members of the crew and one man on the ground. Because the landing had been covered by news cameramen and radio announcers, vivid descriptions and pictures of the disaster quickly circled the globe.

When the explosion aboard the *Hindenburg* occurred, the *Graf Zeppelin* was returning from a trip to Brazil. As soon as the *Graf* was back in Germany, it was retired to its hangar and never permitted to fly commercially again. A brand new airship, named the *Graf Zeppelin II* (LZ-130) was actually completed after the *Hindenburg* disaster and flown a few times, but it was never used to carry paying passengers. Early in 1940, both ships were demolished and later used as scrap by the Germans in World War II.

Since that time, no large rigid airship has been built. The U.S. Navy had some rigid dirigibles of its own, but the last of them, the *Macon,* crashed in 1935. After that the Navy relied on smaller, non-rigid airships, called "blimps." These ships, much like pointed rubber balloons, were used during World War II as antisubmarine patrol and escort craft. Blimps have also been flown as rubber-company advertisements and as long-range platforms for television cameras. But they are only a fraction of the size of the *Graf* or the *Hindenburg,* and there are few of them left.

Will Zeppelins ever fly again? It is perfectly possible, with today's engineering skills, to build a dirigible far larger than the *Hindenburg.* If it were filled with light but nonflammable helium—a gas which the Germans never had—no serious danger of fire would exist. The reason Zeppelins are not being built is that, for most jobs, today's airplanes are better. Huge jets can carry hundreds of passengers across the Atlantic in a few hours, a feat no Zeppelin could match. However, some planners believe that the dream of adapting an atomic power plant to flight could best be done with lighter-than-air ships. For one thing a Zeppelin does not need the enormous power that a plane does to fly. The atomic engine therefore could be smaller, reducing the amount of heavy lead shielding needed for protection against radiation. Such a ship would not have to land for fuel and could remain in the air for many weeks at a time. It could hover over unexplored lands or distant oceans while scientists studied the world and water below. It could transport cargo in countries with few roads, waterways or airplane landing fields.

When the need for any such task becomes great enough to be worth the cost, Count Ferdinand von Zeppelin's invention may yet be reborn, and once again people will look up in awe and watch the huge silver ships sail across the sky.

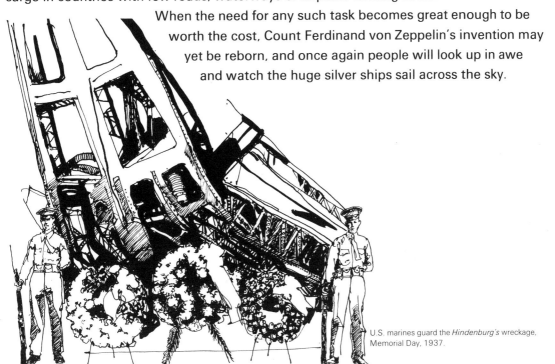

U.S. marines guard the *Hindenburg's* wreckage, Memorial Day, 1937.

Index

Numerals in italics indicate an illustration of the subject mentioned.

Acknowledgments

The artist and editors wish to thank the following for their contributions to this book: Alexander Graf von Brandenstein-Zeppelin, Biberach-Riss, Germany; Isa Gräfin von Brandenstein-Zeppelin, Elm bei Schlüchtern; Hans Scharpf, director of the Stadtisches Bodensee Museum, Friedrichshafen; former Zeppelin personnel: Heinrich Bauer, Eugen Bentele, Ernst Fischbach, Philipp Lenz, Karl Stahl, Karl Rosch, all of Friedrichshafen, and Martin Dietrich of Hamburg; Kurt Puzicha, Erich Rutzen, Hamburg; Tom Keyes, London; Imperial War Museum, London; Dr. Douglas H. Robinson, Trenton, New Jersey; J. Gordon Vaeth, National Environmental Satellite Center, Washington, D.C., and Peter Amesbury, Salzgitter-Lebenstedt, who read and commented on the manuscript; TIME-LIFE correspondents Elisabeth Kraemer, Bonn, and Margot Hapgood, London, and the many people in England and Germany who contributed newspaper clippings and Zeppelin memorabilia.

About the Artist

To gather research for this book, Ken Dallison traveled to Germany, where he interviewed many of the men who worked on and flew the lighter-than-air craft. He culled archives, visited the Zeppelin Museum in Friedrichshafen and talked with retired captains who described their war experiences and memories of the Zeppelin in peacetime. Born in Hounslow, England, Mr. Dallison attended the Twickenham Art School there. He now lives with his family in Locust Valley, New York.